To

Me

From

Me ♡

Date

Started- June 30, 2022

Published by:

21154 Highway 16 East
Siloam Springs, AR 72761
dayspring.com

Written by: Emma Mae McDaniel
Cover Design by: Morgan Morris

Printed in China
Prime: J8528
ISBN: 978-1-64870-795-7

You Are...

Realizing Who You Are Because of Who God Is

EMMA MAE MCDANIEL

DaySpring

LIVE YOUR FAITH

A Note from Emma

Have you ever doubted your worth, felt insecure regarding your purpose, or feared that you weren't loved? Well, if you answered "yes" to any of these questions, I can guarantee you that you are not alone. I have questioned these very things, and I bet that every human on the planet has as well. You were made to have clarity and confidence and assurance when it comes to these foundational questions. The only way, though, that you and I can have assurance when it comes to these questions about who we are is through personally knowing the One who made us.

This inspirational guide may only be thirty days long, but my prayer is that its effects are lifelong. Together, we are going to identify who we are not so that we can replace the lies that have been exposed with the truth. Then, we are going to dive into the truth of who we are. And lastly, we are going to be sent out in the empowering reality of what we were made for. But, as mentioned, we cannot expose the lies, take hold of the truth, and live out the truth if we do not know who God is because He is the truth. So, throughout each chapter we will discover who we really are and where our identity really rests by going to the Bible and learning more and more about who God is, how He made us, and what He made us for.

I am grateful and ecstatic to journey through this inspirational guide with you. I am praying that as you go through this study, the lies that you have believed will break, the truth of who God is will be what your life is built upon, and that this truth that sets you free will burn passionately within your heart as you live it out in boldness each day. I encourage you to pray before you begin each chapter. I challenge you to commit to finishing the study once you begin. I affirm you in desiring to grow and learn, as you have already shown in picking up this book.

For more encouragement you can follow me on Instagram at @1corinthians13_love and tune in to my podcast, *Have You Heard?*

I love you! You are a treasure! Let's grow in truth together!
With Joy, EmmaMae ☺

Contents

YOU ARE...

...NOT HER 9

...NOT THE STRUGGLE 13

...NOT ALONE 17

...NOT ENOUGH 21

...NOT HERE LONG 25

...NOT THE LIKES AND FOLLOWS 29

...NOT THE JUDGE 33

...NOT TOO FAR GONE 37

...NOT YOUR "SUCCESS" 41

...NOT YOUR TITLES 45

...LOVED 49

...KNOWN 53

...ON PURPOSE 57

...PURSUED 61

...TALENTED 65

...UNDERSTOOD 69

...WORTH IT 73

...A SEEKER 77

...BEAUTIFUL 81

...INFLUENTIAL 85

...MADE FOR BETTER 89

...MADE FOR FREEDOM 93

...MADE FOR FRIENDSHIP 97

...MADE FOR JOY 101

...MADE FOR PEACE 105

...MADE TO BE HOLY 109

...MADE TO KEEP GOING 113

...MADE TO LOVE PEOPLE 117

...MADE TO WONDER 121

...MADE TO MAKE HIM KNOWN 125

How do I use this guide?

BEFORE WE GET STARTED

If we are entering a study all about who we are because of who God is, I thought it would be of great importance that we take a moment to acknowledge who God is and why He is the One we can find confidence and secure identity in.

GOD IS... CREATOR AND MAKER

The heavens and the earth were created to be good by God at the start, but He Himself has never begun and never will He end. By His Word, the universe came to be and everything in the earth is His. In the image of Himself, He made you and I fearfully and wonderfully. Every person you see, He knit together within their mother's womb as He saw them in the secret place.

Genesis 1:1 | Psalm 90:2 | Hebrews 11:3 | Colossians 1:15-17 | Genesis 1:27 | Psalm 139:13–16

THREE IN ONE

Throughout this book you will notice that God is referred to as God the Father, God the Son (Jesus), and God the Spirit because all are one in essence and yet have distinct roles. The Father sent His only Son, Jesus. Jesus was on earth as fully God and fully man. He died, was buried, rose on the third day, and now victoriously sits at the right hand of the Father. He is the only way by which we can be saved. The Holy Spirit lives within every one of us who trusts in Jesus, He is where freedom is, and He helps us walk in obedience to the Father.

Matthew 28:19 | Matthew 3:16–17 | John 3:16 | Hebrews 12:2 | I Corinthians 8:6
John 1:14 | I Corinthians 15:3–4 | John 15:26 | II Corinthians 3:17

PERFECT SAVIOR

God is perfect and just in all His ways. Because of His justice and perfection, our disobedience to Him (sin) prevents us from being in relationship with Him as we were made to. This broken relationship brought about brokenness in all our lives and in our world. But God demonstrated His perfect love for us by sending His one and only Son, Jesus, so that we may be in relationship with Him again by grace, through faith. By His perfect means to save us, we can go from brokenness to wholeness as He has desired from the beginning.

Psalm 18:30 | Genesis 3 | Romans 3:23 | John 3:16 | Romans 5:8
Romans 6:23 | Ephesians 2:1–8

TRUTH AND LIFE

So many phrases today are thrown around regarding my truth and your truth, but the real and only truth that brings life and freedom is God Himself. He is the truth, and when we know Him, we are set free. Because He is truth and His Word is breathed out by Him, His Word is truth. His Word never fades away, never changes, and never shifts with the latest trend or opinion. Therefore, we can build our life upon Him with assurance that we cannot be shaken.

We discover abundant life that lasts forever and ever through Jesus Christ alone because He is the life. To know the hope of life forever is to know who God is personally.

John 14:6 | John 8:32 | II Timothy 3:16 | John 17:17 | Matthew 7:24–27 | Psalm 119:160
Hebrews 13:8 | Matthew 24:35 | Numbers 23:19 | I John 5:11–12 | John 11:25–26

ABOVE ALL

No plan the Lord has can be thwarted, for He is above all and holds all authority. He is worthy of all praise and all glory, and nothing is too hard for Him. He sits enthroned as king forever and nothing good is lacking in Him. Jesus has been given all authority, as well as the name that is above every name.

Job 42:2 | Philippians 2:9–11 | Psalm 138:2 | Matthew 28:18 | Ephesians 1:21 | Psalm 145

Thanks for taking the time to read through these foundational truths with me. I am so excited for you to be encouraged in the truth of who you are!

QR CODES

There are six QR codes throughout this inspiration guide. They will lead you to one of my podcast episodes, where you will hear conversations on the very topic you are reading about.

1. Open the camera on your phone.

2. Point the camera at the QR code (the small square barcode-looking, black-and-white box in the bottom right corner). If your front-facing camera is on, first tap the camera-shaped icon to flip it.

3. Make sure the QR code is centered on the camera screen. All four edges of the QR code should be on the screen.

4. Wait for the code to scan. (It should scan almost immediately.)
   Open the QR code's content. Tap the notification that appears at the top of the screen to open the QR code's webpage or other information.

You are not her

I was driving down the road one day and noticed that a couple of cars came from behind me, sped up, and got in front of me. My initial thought was that I was going too slow because of how fast they were going, but as I looked at my speed, I realized that I was indeed going the speed limit. Then this question hit me—why did I automatically assume that I was wrong because I was going at a different pace than someone else?

How often do we do this in life? We glance to our right and to our left to see others moving at a different pace than us or looking different than us, and our initial thought is that we are in the wrong because we aren't the same? We don't act like, talk like, or look like them and immediately assume that we are wrong because of it. The thoughts, I should be doing more, producing more, knowing more . . . pass through our minds, but it's all from a place of thinking we should be where everyone else is rather than acknowledging that God has us right where we are supposed to be and resting in that.

We cannot be confident in who God uniquely made us to be if we are constantly consumed with comparing ourselves to the girl to the right and left of us. We cannot be content in the season that the Lord has us in if we are constantly basing the goodness of the season we are in off of the season that the girl next to us is in. Then, we aren't basing goodness on Who God is, but we are basing goodness on what someone else has or where someone else is. This is a dangerous and exhausting way to live. When the standard of where you should be is the girl to the right or to the left of you, your standard will be unreachable because you were never meant to be the girl to the right or to the left of you. You, in fact, were meant to be you.

Comparing ourselves to others comes from a place of insecurity and pride, which leads not only to us missing out on the goodness of where God has us and how He made us, but we also miss out on a special opportunity to celebrate our sister in a personal way. There will always be opportunities to compare, but this means there will always be opportunities to appreciate the beauty in others and appreciate the beauty in yourself that God placed there on purpose to reflect Who He is as well.

Hebrews 12:2 | II Timothy 2:2 | Galatians 5:26 | John 10:10

In John 10:10, Jesus says that He has come so we may have life and have it to the fullest, but the enemy is the thief who steals, kills, and destroys. One of the ways that I have seen the enemy steal the power of sisterhood, kill confidence, and destroy contentment is working through the seeds of insecurity and pride that produce comparison and divide friendships.

Something that hinders us that the Lord says we should throw off in Hebrews 12 is the habit of comparing ourselves to others in a way that is jealous and insecure. God made us to be in community and to love each other well, but we cannot love each other well and be jealous of each other at the same time.

Scripture says to fix our eyes on Jesus, who is the Author and the Perfecter of our faith. Scripture does not say that we are to fix our eyes on the girl next to us or to the girl on the screen. Jesus is our standard for where we should be and what we should aim for. Who Jesus is and how He lived His life here on earth should be our place of confidence and our compass for knowing whether we are going in the right direction. May we not get caught up in who is better than who, but may we get caught up in celebrating one another and in how we can learn from one another as we look to Jesus.

RESPONSE QUESTIONS

*How have you seen joy and confidence robbed from you
when you are consumed with comparison?*

yes. so often it makes me question everything ~ my decisions, my clothes, my life style

*Instead of comparing yourself to someone else, how can you learn from them
or express appreciation for the beauty in them instead?*

My first thought is of Erika and it's hard because at first I feel prideful; when I remember that God made her I see how helpful & organized she is. She doesn't give up on others easily.

Do you notice that you compare more from a place of pride—thinking you are better than others? Or do you notice that you compare more from a place of insecurity—thinking others are better than you?

Both. When I am away, by myself it's pride but when I am with someone it's insecurity.

How have you seen yourself look to people for the standard of what is good instead of looking to Jesus as the standard of what is good?

Yes.

What are five things you love about how God made you?

1. I have a "get it done attitude"

2. I give as much as I can in all situations

3. I can admit my mistakes / when I'm wrong

4. I grow consistently

5. I am wise (sometimes)

It is powerful when we take the time to sit down and appreciate the qualities in ourselves that God gave us and the qualities in others that God gave to them.

What are five things you love about how God made your friend/coworker/sister?

Brooklyn
Passinate
Quirky   a babbling brook
Supportive
funny   Honest

Angela
a great mom
so calm & peaceful
Caring   a listener

It is quite difficult to genuinely rejoice over how God has uniquely made someone or gifted someone and simultaneously be jealous of them and bitter toward them.

You are not the struggle

To struggle is a part of being human. Something that my mom would sometimes tell me was that I am not special. Now, I know what you may be thinking: Wow, that's harsh. But let me explain where she was coming from and why I needed to hear it. My mom was not speaking down on my confidence, or purpose, or significance. In fact, she was doing the opposite and helping me shift my focus. My mom told me this a couple of times when I came to her explaining something I was struggling with. Typically, this struggle was a fear or worry that was showing itself in overthinking and I was dwelling on it and letting it weigh me down. Something that I wrestle with at times is when I am struggling, the struggle itself becomes a struggle because I convince myself that I am not supposed to struggle; I am supposed to have it all figured out; I am supposed to have life mastered . . . oh goodness, what a hot mess that thought process becomes.

To be special is to be "better, greater, or otherwise different from what is usual." So, to further explain my mom's "you are not special" statement, she was saying exactly what I needed to hear because I was subconsciously believing that I was special in an unrealistic way, that I was different from the usual and better in the fact that I wasn't supposed to struggle like every other human on the planet does, special in the fact that I was supposed to have it all figured out.

Why am I sharing this with you? Because I believe that many of us tie our identity and worth to our struggles because subconsciously, we expect perfection from ourselves—expect ourselves to be special from the rest of humanity and never struggle with anything at all. This in and of itself produces shame because we aren't even giving ourselves permission to be human and have struggles and, therefore, deal with them appropriately.

Shame says that you are what you have done. Condemnation says that you are the mistakes that you have made. As long as we walk in shame and condemnation, we will continue to neglect acknowledging the mistake for what it is, accepting and living in forgiveness, and moving forward in freedom. So, I want to pass on the encouragement to you that you are not the struggle you are currently dealing with, nor are you abnormal for struggling. You are the farthest from alone in this department because as humans, we struggle, simply put. And there is freedom in simply being honest about this rather than expecting perfection.

"Perfectionism is not the same thing as striving to be your best. **✳✳***Perfectionism is the belief that if we live perfect, look perfect, and act perfect, we can minimize or avoid the pain of blame, judgement, and shame.* ✳✳*It's a shield. It's a twenty-ton shield that we lug around thinking it will protect us, when, in fact, it's the thing that's really preventing us from flight."*

LISTEN AND RESPOND

As you listen to or watch the podcast episode "You Are Not the Struggle," fill in the blanks as you go.

To hold yourself to the standard of ___perfection___ is to hold yourself to an unrealistic and defeating standard.

Separating the ___struggles___ from your worth and identity frees you to experience the grace of God and acknowledge your need for Him.

You are ___NOT___ expected to have it all figured out.

___Breath___ and let yourself enjoy getting to learn.

DIVE DEEPER INTO SCRIPTURE

Psalm 34:5 | Romans 8:1

"The looked to him and were radiant, and their faces were not ashamed"

"There is now no condemnation to those who are in Christ Jesus"

Write down moments that you know you tend to be harder on yourself.

Mothering & being a wife, sinning when my mistake affect those I love the most. God → husband → kids

With these situations in mind, what are the thoughts that typically run through your mind? What are the thought patterns that repeat themselves? It could be:

I am such a failure.
I can never do anything right.
They will never see me the same or like me again.

ALL

Do the thoughts seem to play off of each other like this? Well, if so, know that you are not alone. I have had those same thought patterns too, but these thought patterns cannot stay. They have had their time of taking you captive, and now it is time for you to take them captive and make them obedient to what is actually true (II Corinthians 10:5). A consistent thought pattern of lies is not going to stop swirling around your mind and taking deeper root until you purposefully rebuke it and replace it with the truth. So, that's what we are going to do today.

The Word of God that teaches us what is true, corrects us in how we see ourselves and how we see grace, rebukes the false thought patterns we have believed, and trains us to live out this transformed way of thinking.

Write down one verse below that refers to what God says about grace and shame.

Hebrews 10:22 Let us draw near to God with a sincere heart and with the full assurance that faith brings, having our hearts sprinkled to cleanse us from a guilty conscience and having our bodies washed with pure water.

Now devote yourself to memorizing this verse. Maybe even write it on a sticky note and put it somewhere you will see it every day. We cannot change our way of thinking if we do not make a change in our day-to-day living. Make the choice to see healthy change by hiding God's Word in your heart and believing what He says about you and His grace toward you through Jesus.

you are not alone

I don't know if you have experienced this too, but when I throw my hair up in a bun, I desire for it to be messy and put together. I am very strategic in trying to make just the right pieces stick out and just the right pieces tucked in. It's kind of funny that this hairstyle is called a "messy bun," yet, it's only supposed to look as messy as I want it to.

I think this is a lot like our conversations with each other sometimes, meaning that we talk about the tough stuff but only to the extent at which we believe that the other person still perceives us as "put together." We let some information about who we are stick out, but we tuck away the information that we think would make us look too messed up, just as we do with our hair when putting up a messy bun.

This is a very dangerous and a very lonely way to go about life, and the enemy thrives on it. When we are convinced that no one would see us or love us the same if they knew about all the pieces of hair that we have tucked away, we head down the road of believing the lie that we are all alone. The enemy schemes to convince us that no one else could ever possibly understand what we are going through. He would love for us to keep the struggles and hurts to ourselves and convince us that living in secrecy is the best and safest route we have. Secrecy is where shame dwells and healing is prevented.

We all battle thoughts like, *No one will think of me the same once they know about* *this thing I struggle with* or, *No one will understand or relate to me.* But these thought processes can make us miss out on so much joy in relationships. We are not alone at all because there are people everywhere going through such similar things, yet we live as though we are all alone because we don't do life with each other.

Not only are we not alone, but we were not designed by God to walk through life alone. When we try to take on life all by ourselves, we will—without a doubt—get exhausted, because trying to make sure our lives look like the perfect kind of "put together" is choosing to live a life that we were never handmade by God to live.

I am not saying that you should go tell everyone everything about your life, but I am encouraging you to evaluate your life and who you are walking through it with. Are there girls in your life who know about the hair you have tucked away? In other words, do you have girls in your life who know you on a deeper level and love you? Are you doing life in community? Because, sister, until you are honest with trusted people about your journey, then the lie that you are all alone is only going to fester. When we believe the lie that we are all alone, we live as though we are all alone. Don't keep exhausting yourself to maintain an image that bears a weight you were never meant to carry and keeps you from the joy of doing life with people.

"Shame hates it when we reach out and tell our story. It hates having words wrapped around it—it can't survive being shared. Shame loves secrecy. When we bury our story, the shame metastasizes."

LISTEN AND RESPOND

As you listen to or watch the podcast episode "You Are Not Alone," fill in the blanks as you go.

To _try & manage_ messy and put together after a while will drive us to _exhauster._

When we refuse to go beyond _surface level_ with our trusted people, we are actually refusing to experience the truth that we are not alone.

When we believe the lie that we are all _alone_, we begin to live as though we are all _alone_.

When _____ is met with _____, a safe place is cultivated and lies are replaced with the truth.

DIVE DEEPER INTO SCRIPTURE

Galatians 6:2 | Proverbs 27:17
Ecclesiastes 4:9–12 | Isaiah 41:10

RESPONSE QUESTIONS

Describe how it makes you feel when you imagine someone knowing the tougher stuff in your life? Why do you think it makes you feel this way?

panicked, scared and ashamed, Fear of losing relationships

What are the things in your life that keep you in shame because you let them remain hidden and tucked away?

my bouts of rage, my mothering mistakes, my confusion or mis understanding

How are you encouraged knowing that there is blessing, joy, and freedom on the other side of vulnerability with your trusted community?

It is such an encouragement knowing that we all struggle & we can support one another through the struggle, the rejoice

When sisterhood or community is mentioned, who comes to your mind? together *Write down their names and send them a text or give them a call, telling them how much you love and appreciate them and the safe place your relationship is.*

Brooklynn ☑   Lisa ☑
Angela ☑   ♡love

If no particular name comes to mind, below, write out a prayer to God. Thank Him for comforting you today in the truth that you are not alone and that you were made to be known and loved and to do life with people. Pray that He will open your eyes to see the people whom you can have a deep and trusting relationship with, and pray that He will give you the courage to be honest and not keep parts of your life tucked away in shame.

Dear Lord, Thank you for providing real friendships for me when I was alone! you've opened the door to community for me, hold my hand as I take the first steps in following the life you've created for me. Amen

You are not enough

Okay. I know that this title appears to be the opposite of encouragement. You may have even read the title of this chapter a couple of times, thinking, Is this a typo? Please, let me explain, because this is not a chapter where I am saying that you are not loved as you are or that you need to work harder or strive more to be accepted. Please hear me when I say that, "You are not enough" actually is meant to uplift you and relieve you greatly.

We live in a world where to be motivated is to be hyped-up in what you can achieve and how you can perform. While it is very important to give our all and work hard, it is important to not have this mentality when it comes to being saved by God. Once we get into the mentality that we can achieve enough for God to love us or we can perform at a certain level for God to save us, then we have missed the message of the Gospel. The Gospel is not a display of how we did enough of something to have earned God's love or achieved a high enough number of good deeds, and therefore, are now being rewarded by the gift of grace and eternity with God.

I love in Ephesians 2 where Paul says, it is by grace we have been saved, through faith. This is not of our works, so we cannot boast, but it is in fact a gift from God. So, it really isn't how much I can achieve or how well I can perform that causes me to be loved by God or saved from the death that I deserve because of sin. I could never do enough good things, perform at enough impressive levels, or achieve enough applause to earn God's approval.

It is simply by grace and through faith in Jesus.

So, when I say that you are not enough, I am not saying this to discourage you, but rather I pray that these words relieve you of the unhelpful pressure to earn what God is simply wanting to freely give to you. I pray that you know that we could never be good enough to be saved by God, yet He demonstrated His perfect love for us anyway in that while we were still sinners, Christ died for us. Through faith in Jesus, the pressure of meeting a standard we could never meet has been relieved by the Lord on our behalf, and this relief compels us to live in such a way that shows God how grateful we are for such a gift.

Ephesians 2:8–9 | II Corinthians 12:9
Romans 6:23 | Romans 3:24

RESPONSE QUESTIONS

In what ways are you seeking to earn God's approval through how you live?

Describe how you feel knowing that Christ is enough for you?

What does it say about God that He is enough when you can't be?

How does this understanding of the Gospel excite you to live differently?

Either using words or pictures, describe the relief you feel knowing that you no longer have to strive to earn the love of God because His love is a free gift to you through Christ.

You are not here long

We have so much anticipation built toward moments, and before we know it, we are reflecting on them saying, "Remember when?" or "Goodness, that went fast!" In the moments and anticipations of life, we don't see the quickness of them, but we think about how fast time flew by pretty much every time we look back on them. Though in the moment this may be hard to believe, our life truly goes by like a blink of an eye in comparison to the length of eternity. James said that our life is like the morning fog—it's here a little while, and then it's gone.

My dad has encouraged me in more ways than one, and I truly think I could write an entire book of all the godly advice he has shared with me. One of these pieces of advice was when he told me about the four *W's*. They represent four different groups of people that we find ourselves in, which consist of the Wishers, the Waiters, the Watchers, and the Workers.

The Wishers are the people who wish their life away, and they neglect making the most of the moment they are in because they are constantly wishing they were in the next one. The Waiters never get to work because they are waiting on the "perfect moment" without realizing that the "perfect moment" to be obedient to the Lord and love people and serve wholeheartedly and walk by faith is right now. The Watchers do exactly that—they watch. They watch life go by because they allow fear or apathy to take each moment captive. The Workers are the ones who go and make the most of the life they have been given. When I think of the Workers, I think of the verse that says, "This is the day that the Lord has made, we will rejoice and be glad in it." (Psalm 118:24 NKJV). Because they know that the breath in their lungs is from the Lord and the day they have to live is from the Lord, they will live like that is true.

God has given us this very day as a gift, and we are to make the most of it in obedience to Him. We are not promised another day here on earth, but we do have right now, and I know that out of all four *W's*, I want to be known for being a faithful Worker.

To know my life is _____ in comparison to _____ motivates me to make the most of my time while I am here.

When I find myself _____ for the perfect time to make the most of my opportunities, I need to ask myself how I am defining "_____."

The work of God is not_____, but it is_____it.

DIVE DEEPER INTO SCRIPTURE

James 4:13-14 | Matthew 6:34 | Psalm 90:12 | Ephesians 5:16

RESPONSE QUESTIONS

Out of the four W's mentioned, which one do you relate to the most? Why?

How does it make you feel knowing that another day here on earth is not a guarantee? Does it make you want to reprioritize or be more intentional?

What would change about your life if you started to live each day wanting to make it count for God?

Have you surrendered your life to the Lord?

This is the best next step in making today count. God tells us in His Word that we aren't promised another day here on earth, and it is only through faith in Jesus that we shall be saved. Don't be a Waiter and think a better moment is going to come for you to surrender to the Lord.

Scripture says that God ordained every day of our lives before a single one of them came to be, so He knows what each day holds and is great at guiding us through them. But, He doesn't force us to follow His guidance. He lets us choose how we spend our time and where our focus will be. Will we choose to work wholeheartedly for Him and make the most of this gift of life He has given us? Or will we be Wishers, Waiters, and Watchers? He lets us choose, but He also clearly lets us know what the best choice is.

Fill each Polaroid with words or pictures, telling or showing different ways to be a Worker who makes the most use of her time today.

(Different ideas for each polaroid could be an act of kindness, spending time in God's Word, saying something encouraging to a stranger, taking time to pray, putting down your phone to be fully present with the person you're with, getting a task done that has been put off for a while, etc.)

To begin a life of intentional work takes one decision to:
not wish away but fully engage | not wait for perfect but step out and do it now
not watch but be a part of

You are not the likes and follows

I'm pretty confident when I say that I am not the only one who gets encouraged when people like my posts and choose to follow me. I would also confidently say that I am not the only one who gets her feelings hurt sometimes when people write mean comments and choose to unfollow me.

When I think about likes and follows, many things come to mind, but one thing in particular is the word inconsistent. I remember one time I was streaming on Instagram Live, and within seconds I had someone tell me that I was hideous and someone else tell me that I was beautiful. If I believe deep down that I am defined by what people have to say about me, then in that very moment I am thrown into total confusion as to who I am and what my worth is.

My mother-in-law once shared with me that there are times when we need to be rubber and other times when we need to be a sponge. When she explained this statement, she said that basically there will be times when I hear words from people that I need to let bounce off of me and not take ownership of. At other times, there will be words that people share that I do need to receive and heed to. If I don't have the discernment between when to soak up words versus when to disregard them, I very easily could take hold of words and opinions that are not mine to keep. I believe we do this a lot with likes and follows on social media. We are sponges to every comment, every follow, and every like. But because we are sponges to these things, we are also sponges to every unfollow and every dislike.

When I believe that my identity is associated with whether people like me and follow me, I will live for the approval of people. I will post only what I think everyone will like. I will dress only how I think everyone is expecting me to dress. I will say only what everyone desires for me to say. And not too long into this direction, I am exhausted. I get exhausted because this burden of seeking to please every human is a burden that I was never designed to carry and an expectation I can never possibly meet.

What is your honest response to the likes or dislikes of people? Does the approval of people hold more weight on your heart than the approval of the Lord?

Galatians 1:10 | John 12:43
Proverbs 29:25

RESPONSE QUESTIONS

When we are soaking up one thing, we are rubber to another. We cannot soak up and live on every opinion people have of us AND the Word of God. We either let words that are not from Him bounce off, or we let words that are from Him bounce off—but we cannot possibly do both.

What words have you been soaking up like a sponge and what words have you been letting bounce off?

What impact have these words or lack thereof had on your life?

If you were to be honest, are you making decisions with the desire to be approved by people or to be approved by God? What words are holding the most weight in your life?

When I _____ every opinion people have, I am setting myself up for _____.

Sometimes I need to be _____, and other times I need to be a _____.

We must get to a place where the approval of _____ drives our decision-making.

We _____ others better when we aren't _____ for their approval.

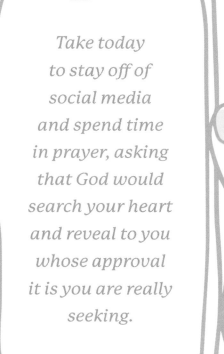

Take today to stay off of social media and spend time in prayer, asking that God would search your heart and reveal to you whose approval it is you are really seeking.

You are not the judge

How often is it that we assume everything about a person before simply taking the time to get to know them? How often do we conclude whether someone is cool enough to be with us within seconds of looking at them? Whether it's stalking someone's Instagram feed or simply seeing someone walk by, in an instant we form our opinions about them and let those opinions be what determine how we treat them. When we spend time concluding who is good enough to have our attention and who is not, we are simply not loving people.

Instead of looking at the person to our right and to our left and making conclusions about who they are and what they may or may not deserve, may we be quick to make the conclusion that we are to love them anyway. It is very likely that we do not know the details of their story and where they have been and how it is that they got to where they are, but we shouldn't need to know any of these details to decide whether we are to love them or not.

When we are quick to assume everything about someone, we are allowing walls of judgement to be built, causing a potential relationship with that person to be torn down. I love to look at the life of Jesus and see whom He met with and sat with and built relationships with on purpose. Even a glance at His disciples alone gives a hint at the kind of person Jesus was. His everyday crew of guys included a tax collector that many despised and your average fishermen. He stopped to engage with the sick, the poor, the overlooked, and the outcast. He didn't have the mentality that He was too important to look in the eyes of any other person and have a conversation with them.

To judge is "to form an opinion or conclusion about," and we can be all too quick to determine whether someone is worthy of our respect or kindness. This simply cannot be our filter as children of God. No matter who someone is or how different someone may look or where someone is from, they are to be loved. Why? Because Christ first loved us. And who knows, God may use your boldness to put aside assumptions to inspire others to do the same. You never know how your boldness could encourage others.

judge

/ jəj /

verb

to form an opinion or conclusion about

———

DIVE DEEPER INTO SCRIPTURE

Matthew 7
Judge not, lest you too be judged

James 2
Showing no partiality

RESPONSE QUESTIONS

Describe a time you formed an opinion about someone before taking the time to know them? How did you treat them?

Describe a time when someone formed an opinion about you without knowing you, and treated you according to that opinion? How did that make you feel?

How are you challenged by God's Word that says to not judge others and to love them no matter what?

Seek out the best in people today. Love the person you normally are quick to judge. Form this conclusion about those you encounter today: they are loved. No, they may not have the same style as you, they may not have the best reputation, they may not be the popular one . . . but they are loved. Let that conclusion alone be the filter you use in how you treat them. Then, come back to this page and write down how it went—what was hard, what was easier than you thought, how did they respond, etc.

you are not too far gone

"No matter what their diseases were, the touch of his hand healed every one."

— LUKE 4:40 NLT

It is so easy to look at the lives of others and hear their stories—what they have been through, what they have learned from, how they have struggled, and where they are now—and go into comparison mode. It is quite easy to quickly think about how much it makes sense that God would have healed them and restored them, but in no way could He possibly do the same to me because my story and struggles are far worse and not able to be forgiven (so my mind thinks). Somehow, we are convinced that the mistakes we have made are beyond the work of what God did on the cross, which reveals our misunderstanding of what the cross represents.

For example, I could hear someone talking about their struggles from the past and how the Lord has saved them and brought freedom to their life that was once in bondage. But in an instant, my mind goes to how different I am. I begin to think about how I have been living a life of constant worry and fear and God may have been able to do a mighty work in their life, but because I believe my struggle is worse, I don't think God can change my life and still love me as He does others. Sometimes, at least for me, I can listen to the stories of other people and immediately go to a thought pattern of how much worse of a person I am. As crazy as this sounds, so many of us think and believe in this way.

Whether it's a addiction, constant jealousy and comparison, worry and fear gone wild, or lying all the time, the Lord is faithful and just to forgive us and cleanse us of all unrighteousness when we confess our sins to Him (I John 1:9). As today's verse says, "No matter what their diseases were, the touch of his hand healed every one." No matter what your life has looked like, no matter how far away you have run, no matter all the things that you said you would never do and did anyway—the touch of Jesus is able and willing to heal you. You are not too far gone. You are not worse than the person next to you who is experiencing a life of freedom. That same freedom is still fully available to you because Jesus came to save the whole world—anyone who believes—not just some. You are not too far gone, and God made a way for you to be near Him.

Luke 15:11–32 | *Parable of the Prodigal Son*

II Peter 3:9 | *The Lord is patient, not wanting anyone to perish.*

RESPONSE QUESTIONS

Do you find yourself comparing your past to the past of the person next to you?

Why is it that you believe your mistakes are different than everyone else? Why do you believe that you are outside of God's grace and forgiveness?

What does it say about God that He would make a way for you to be forgiven no matter what your history has been?

WRITE OUT THESE VERSES BELOW

I John 1:9

Ephesians 1:7

Now, take the verses that you wrote out above, and write them again below. This time, though, include your name in it.

For example:

"If Emma confesses her sins, He is faithful and just to forgive her sins and to cleanse her from all unrighteousness."

Now you try, and don't just know it in your head but believe it wholeheartedly!

you are not your "success"

You know those statements you hear or conversations you have that just stick with you and challenge you in a good way? I had one of those conversations with my uncle one day. He began to tell me about two people from the Bible: Jeremiah and Jonah.

He reviewed both of their stories with me, sharing how Jeremiah was called by God to be a messenger of what God wanted to communicate to the people of Israel. This message was no easy one, for the people of Israel were rebelling against the Lord. Jeremiah was the man for the job of telling them to stop what they were doing and turn to God . . . not a popular message nor one the people wanted to hear. And even though it brought opposition and persecution, Jeremiah was obedient to God. He was obedient to God even when not a single person listened to what Jeremiah was saying and ultimately, not a single person turned away from their disobedience.

At a different time, Jonah was also called by God to communicate a message to the people of Nineveh who were living in sin. Jonah was to go to Nineveh and, like Jeremiah, tell the people to turn from their evil ways and surrender to God. Jonah, however, was disobedient and hopped on a boat to go in a different direction than Nineveh. After a crazy story of being swallowed by a fish and spit up on the shore of Nineveh, Jonah finally preached to the people that they needed to turn to God and away from the way they were living. The people of Nineveh, unlike the people of Israel, listened to Jonah's message from God and they turned from their evil ways and surrendered before the Lord.

Now, looking at these two stories, which one would you say is the successful one? More than likely you would probably say that Jonah was the most successful because the people listened to him and responded well. What may surprise you, though, is that my uncle said Jeremiah was most successful—not because of the response he got from people but because of his obedience to God the first time (he didn't initially run away from his assignment, but instead he immediately embraced it).

I put "success" in quotation marks because it is important for us to define what we think success is. Do we have a "Jonah" perspective of success or a "Jeremiah" perspective? Are we aiming for success with the understanding of success being how many people like us or how much money we receive or whether we get the promotion? Or, are we aiming for success with the understanding that success is encouraging the person I am standing next to or sharing the Gospel with? We are all aiming for success, but how are we defining it? Our success doesn't define who we are, but it does reveal where we believe our source of identity to be. When we see success as obedience to the Lord, it is made clear that we know our identity is in the Lord because it is the Lord who drives our desire to succeed.

Refer to passages from Jeremiah and Jonah's life.

RESPONSE QUESTIONS

*Up until now, would you say you have more of a
"Jeremiah perspective" or "Jonah perspective" of success?*

How would your life look different if you saw obedience to God as success?

What does it say about God that when we are obedient, He sees that as success?

*Are you willing to sacrifice earthly success (popularity, promotions, more stuff)
if it means eternal success through obedience to God?*

With "Jeremiah's perspective" of success, what are some practical ways that you can be successful today?

You are not your titles

And David realized that the Lord had confirmed him as king over Israel and had greatly blessed his kingdom for the sake of his people Israel.

— I CHRONICLES 14:2 NLT

I came naked from my mother's womb, and I will be naked when I leave. The Lord gave me what I had, and the Lord has taken it away. Praise the name of the Lord!

— JOB 1:21 NLT

I remember a few years ago that my dad approached me and said, "If every title you have were to be taken away from you (daughter, sister, author, speaker, girlfriend, etc.) who are you?"

I sat as he shared with me that I am a child of God. He spoke over me that I belong to the Lord and am loved by Him and am here to glorify His Name, no matter what title here on earth I have or do not have. David and Job grasped this very well. I love how it says in Scripture that David "realized" who gave him the title he had and why it was entrusted to him. He "realized" that it was the Lord who gave him his title and it was for the purpose of blessing people. Job, in a different way but with the same heart, had his titles stripped from him, yet he praised the Lord. How could he do this? Because he knew that the Lord was in control and that his identity was not rooted in the things of this world that are here one day and then gone the next. Job knew that his identity was in the Lord who was worthy of his praise no matter how the titles came and went.

When we realize that it is the Lord who gives us the titles we have for the purpose of blessing people, we will handle the titles differently. We will handle them with the filters of, "What brings honor to the Lord?" and "How can I use this to serve people?" When we are convinced that our titles are all about us and for us and because of us, we handle them with the filters of, "What brings the most benefit to me?" or "I am nothing without this relationship, job, etc." When our identity is in our titles, we are fully thrown into complete chaos and uncertainty regarding who we are when these titles are removed. Whereas, when our identity is in what God says about us, our confidence doesn't have to disappear when our titles do.

Go read more of the story about David in I Chronicles 14. I know you'll find it to be so powerful and encouraging!

RESPONSE QUESTIONS

What titles do you currently hold?

Do you realize that God has entrusted these titles to you to glorify Him and bless people? Does this change the way you view these titles?

If all these titles were to be taken away, who are you still?

You may even be wondering what it means for your identity to be in the Lord. Well, your identity is who you are—it is what makes you, you. So, all of us have been made in God's image and were made by Him, but when we don't trust that who we are is defined by our Maker we will trust that something else defines us and live like that to be true. That is why we are walking through all these chapters—to bring clarity to who you are not, who you are, and what you were made for.

So, whether or not you know God, the source of who you are is in Him because He made you and there is simply no escaping that. But, when you put your faith in Jesus, you have an identity in Christ. This means that you are a new creation, a child of God, and the list goes on. Our identity in Jesus Christ is unchanging and secure. This is what I mean by being able to remain confident even when our titles come and go—it's because Christ does not come and then go. He is with those who call upon His Name and never leaves them nor forsakes them. This security in identity is available to you right now.

Based on these verses below, what titles do we have in Christ that never go away?

HELLO MY NAME IS

II CORINTHIANS 5:17

1 PETER 2:9

JOHN 1:12

EPHESIANS 2:10

JOHN 15:15

ROMANS 8:17

EPHESIANS 1:7

ROMANS 8:37

II CORINTHIANS 5:21

MATTHEW 5:14

you are loved

Before my husband, Josh, and I began dating, I was having a difficult time trusting God's love for me. It was a tough and confusing time. It is so cool to me, though, how God meets us where we are and encourages us exactly how we need. That's what happened when God brought Josh into my life. Because it was through and still is through my relationship with Josh that the Lord continues to remind me of His character and who I am in Him over and over again.

Marriage is such a cool way God shows us what our relationship with Him is like. I am coming to know the love of God more as I walk through this relationship with Josh. One of the big reasons I say this is because Josh has seen me through a lot. He has seen me through many celebrations as well as many low points. He has seen me when at my best, and he has heard me express my deepest fears. He has seen me through all this and more, and still he got down on one knee and asked if he could be committed to me for the rest of our lives. Still to this day that amazes me, and I believe it will for the rest of my life. How is it that someone can see the flaws and shortcomings and imperfections in me and still so passionately and confidently choose me? I specifically use this word choose because Josh didn't have to commit to me but willingly decided to do so. And even as I type that, I understand that I too have seen Josh's highs and lows, and still I choose him on purpose because I love him. It is a two-way display of unconditional love that points to the heart of God.

As fantastic as this all sounds, I still am sometimes not as quick to be encouraged in hearing that God loves me because I tend to be harder on myself. So, if I have a hard time being loving and gracious toward myself in the moments that I fail, how on earth can the Lord, who is perfect and holy, love me? This is the insanely beautiful and deep love of God. Even when it doesn't make sense to us, it doesn't change the fact that it's still true. He chooses us when we don't give Him reason to. He confidently declared that He desires a forever relationship with us through sending His one and only Son, Jesus. Just as Josh and I are aware of each other's faults and still chose one another, God knows our shortcomings, yet, in His wealth of mercy and kindness, still chose us. We are so loved by God.

John 3:16 | Romans 8:37–39
Romans 5:8 | Ephesians 2:4–5
Psalm 136:26 | I John 4:8

RESPONSE QUESTIONS

Do you have a difficult time trusting the love that God has for you?
Why do you think that is?

What does it say about God that He would love us even though we have all messed up?

In what ways can you practice trusting God's love for you today?

Color and doodle on the next page
as you meditate on God's promises.

John 3:16

I am loved

you are known

Have you ever gotten ready for the day or for a special event in front of one of those mirrors that magnify every pore, eyebrow hair, and freckle? It's like if you didn't know it was a part of your facial feature, then now you do. Those mirrors really get up close and personal. Sometimes I have wished I had a different mirror so that all those details weren't so magnified. It can make me uncomfortable seeing myself that close and being made aware of blackheads on my nose. But from a different perspective, I am thankful to admire a freckle that I hadn't noticed before or to pluck an eyebrow hair that just had to go. There is awkward discomfort in those mirrors sometimes, yet they are good because I get to see my face for all of what it is.

In a deeper way, like the mirror, God knows us at a greater depth than what we even know about ourselves. He is the very one who made us. He knows every joy we have shared with our friends and every sound of laughter that has ever crossed our lips. He knows every single tear we have shed. He knows what gets us excited and what brings us sadness and what gets under our skin. He knows the thoughts we have each had and the very motive of why we do what we do. He knew us within our mother's womb before anyone else on earth knew of our name. Talk about being up close and personal!

Reading this may make you feel like how the close-up mirror makes you feel. You could be feeling discomfort at the thought of God knowing everything about you. Or you could be filled with gratitude as you are reading about how much He sees and knows you personally. Just as the details of your face in the mirror are brought to attention and taken note of in the magnified mirror, so are the details of who you are brought to the attention of the Father because He cares about you. You are not simply another person walking the face of the earth; you are a person known fully by the God who made the heavens and the earth. He isn't intimidated by the blackheads or the eyebrow hairs that haven't yet been plucked in our lives. Hopefully, knowing that He already knows, you are encouraged to talk with the Lord and share with Him what is on your heart.

In Psalm 139: 1—5 (ESV), David says,

"O Lord, you have searched me and known me! You know when I sit down and when I rise up; you discern my thoughts from afar. You search out my path and my lying down and are acquainted with all my ways. Even before a word is on my tongue, behold, O Lord, you know it altogether. You hem me in, behind and before, and lay your hand upon me."

RESPONSE QUESTIONS

Does it make you uncomfortable or encouraged knowing that the Lord sees you and knows you fully?

Why is that?

What does it say about God that He would want to know the details about us?

In the devo, we talked about how the mirror magnifies some things that we don't like to see. Are there things in your life that you don't like to see, and you haven't brought them before the Lord yet?

We also talked about how the mirror points out things we do like to see. What are some things about yourself you didn't know and now love because God has shown them to you as you have walked with Him?

Have a conversation today with the person who knows you the most, the person who has seen your goofy side and knows what makes you laugh, the person who can list story after story from your life and knows the silly and personal things that very few people know.

After this conversation, come back and write out how that made you think about the depth at which God must know you. If He knows you better than anyone else, how personal of a God He must be!

You are on purpose

Thinking about purpose makes me think about the items in my kitchen. The silverware and the coffeepot and the pans and the mixer do not simply sit on the counter or in the cabinet to look nice and fill space. They all have a use and help make amazing dishes. My mixer has helped me make bread and brownies. The coffeepot is filled every morning for Josh and me to enjoy. The silverware helps me enjoy a good bowl of ice cream or the amazing spaghetti and meatballs Josh just made. Yes, I understand that this is a "well, duh" kind of picture to paint here, but thinking about this encouraged me in the reality that you and I are not here on earth to simply look nice and fill space. Just like the mixer was designed with the purpose to make many delicious goodies, so were you and I designed with the purpose to do amazing things.

There have been times when I wrestled with truly believing that my life had purpose. I have had those moments of questioning whether what I was doing mattered and if any of it held significance. These are legitimate questions that every human faces. From the very beginning, Satan has been a questioner of what God said and what God meant. In Genesis 3, he approached Eve in the Garden of Eden asking her if God really said what He did. I believe that he is still a question asker but not out of a desire to know the answer for himself but rather out of a desire for insecurity toward who God is and what He says to take root in our hearts. I have seen this scheme tried many times through the questioning of, "Do you really have purpose?" or "Is God's plan for your life really that significant?" or "Does your life really matter?" The answer to all these questions is yes, yes, and yes. Yet, we can be so quickly discouraged and easy to convince otherwise when we do not know what is true and choose to stand on it. Mark Twain said, "The two most important days of your life are the day you were born and the day you figured out why." This is so because not only is your life important, but for you to believe that to be true is extremely important too.

To think about purpose is to think about the "why" behind what is. Purpose is "the reason for which something is done or created or for which something exists." Other words used to describe purpose are "planned, usefulness, value, reason, and intention." So, when we hear that we have purpose, may we hear that we were made for a reason; the giving of breath to our lungs and a beat to our heart was not accidental; and we have use and value because our existence here on earth is intentional. Now let's go and live like we know our lives to be important.

Psalm 138:8 | Psalm 57:2
Ephesians 2:10 | Jeremiah 29:11
Psalm 139 | Job 42:2

RESPONSE QUESTIONS

*All the Scripture above points to God being a purposeful God.
How does that encourage you knowing that a purposeful God made you?*

*Describe how it makes you feel knowing that you are not the only one
who has wrestled with confidently knowing that you have purpose.*

*Using the Scripture above, how can you now respond to the enemy
when he questions you to create doubt and confusion?*

What does it mean to live like your life is important?

Aunt Katie's Bread

One of my favorite things to make in the kitchen is my Aunt Katie's bread! This recipe will make batches of dough for two loaves, so if you only want one, just cut everything in half (besides the yeast, that is the same).

- 4 tablespoons sugar
- 1 pack of active dry yeast (If you have a jar of yeast, then the pack is equivalent to 2 1/4 teaspoons of yeast from the jar.)
- 2 cups hot (but not boiling) water

Mix these together in a bowl with a mixer until all combined. Let it sit until it gets nice and bubbly/frothy looking.

Next, add:
- 1/2 cup oil
- 1 teaspoon salt
- About a tablespoon of honey
- 5–6 cups of flour (Start with 5 and add 1/4 cup more as needed until dough forms a ball around dough hook and cleans the inside of the bowl.)

Once you add the flour, turn the mixer on low and let it go (adding more flour as needed) until you get the dough ball. Turn mixer up a notch and let it knead the dough for 3 to 5 minutes.

Next, turn the dough out on a surface, grease your mixer bowl, and put the dough back in. Cover and let sit for about 90 minutes until it doubles in size.

Once 90 minutes have passed and the dough has risen, punch dough down (like actually punch it), turn the dough back out onto the surface, and split in two if making two loaves. Next, fold the dough and shape into loaves. There are many videos on YouTube and Pinterest for how to do this.

Put each shaped loaf into a loaf pan, cover, and let it rise for about an hour.

While that is happening, preheat the oven to 350°F. Once the hour is up, put loaf pans into the oven and cook for 30 minutes until top is golden. (Your home is about to smell SO good).

Turn the bread out onto a cooling rack and let it cool for at least 1 hour before cutting into it. When you do cut into it, cut down the middle so it stays fresh longer by putting cut end to cut end. Also, when storing it, you can either wrap it in plastic wrap or put it in a linen bread bag!

After sending this recipe, my Aunt Katie said, "Give it a try or go and pick one of your favorite recipes off of Pinterest and make something yummy today!" And I hope that that is what you do today too!

Take note of how every kitchen item you used played a role into making something amazing, and be encouraged in the same way—you have purpose, and God designed your life to do amazing things!

you are pursued

It feels good to be noticed. I remember when I first noticed that Josh was flirting with me. It made me feel special when Josh asked me on a date and when he bought me flowers and when he wanted to sit next to me. He was pursuing me. In many little and big ways, he was communicating that he wanted me and cared about me. On our wedding day, Josh vowed to never stop dating me. He meant that he was going to continue to pursue me and let me know how special I am to him for as long as we live.

David says in Psalm 23:6 (CSB) that "only goodness and faithful love will pursue me all the days of my life." This word pursue in the Hebrew language means "to run after." It also happens to be the same Hebrew word for persecutor that David and Jeremiah used when asking the Lord to save them from those who were seeking to destroy them. If you are like me in this moment, then you feel like that sentence took a weirdly aggressive turn too, but stay with me. If this word pursue was the same word used to describe those who were intently chasing after David and Jeremiah, then this must be a very powerful word. This is no aimless or passive type of pursuit but rather an on-purpose and active chase.

So, with the meaning of this word in mind, Scripture says that God's goodness and faithful love pursues us all the days of our lives. The Lord intently chases after us but not with the intent for evil as David and Jeremiah's enemies did. The Lord pursues us with His goodness and faithful love. The Lord notices us, and He never tires of pursuing us and communicating in big and little ways that we are on His mind. The way that Josh pursues me is a glimpse of how the Lord pursues us every single day of our life.

But it is important to note that Josh and I did not get married simply because Josh pursued me and wanted me. Yes, that was a major part, but I also had to respond. I had to decide if I wanted to be in a relationship with him and whether or not I was going to commit to him too. In the same way, God has made it known to us that He wants us by sending His one and only Son, Jesus, to save us from the power of sin that leads us to be forever separated from Him. Each of us have the opportunity to respond to this love that is the greatest pursuit mankind will ever know, and our responses to this pursuit of God will change not only our life here on earth but our eternity forever.

Psalm 23:6
Write the Scripture below.

RESPONSE QUESTIONS

Describe how you feel when someone shows that they see you and care about you.

What does it say about God that He would pursue you so intentionally?

What does it say about you that God would want you so dearly?

How will you respond to God's pursuit of you?

*At the end of the day, come back to this page and
write out simple ways that you noticed how God cares for you,
sees you, and pursues you . . .*

you are talented

There is a quote by Jackie Hill Perry that I just love! She says, "You really don't have to excel at everything. That's some unnecessary pressure, my friends. Simply put, just be good at what you're good at."

I am nowhere near good at everything, and I can prove that to you quite quick, but there is a handful of things that I know I do very well. I don't say this in a prideful attitude but rather in a confident and aware attitude. I believe it to be extremely important that we know what we are good at and we seek to grow in those areas and serve others through those areas. These talents that each of us have are given to us by the Lord, and when we know that and believe that He designed us to be good at those things, we are motivated to steward them well.

There is a parable in Matthew 25 that Jesus tells regarding what the kingdom of heaven will be like, and it is about a man who entrusted different parts of his property to three of his servants. To one servant he gave five talents, to another servant he gave two talents, and to another servant he gave one talent. The first two servants went to make more talents off the ones they already had, but the third servant who had received one talent hid what he was given because he was afraid of losing it. The man who entrusted the one talent to him was not pleased when he returned because he did not steward faithfully what was given to him. He didn't use what he had.

What talents and skills have been given to you by God? What are you good at? Do you invest in getting better at these things? Do you seek opportunities to practice these strengths? If not, why? Are you afraid like the third servant was? Maybe you are not necessarily afraid that you are going to lose it, but are you afraid that you won't be good enough and therefore you never try? Are you afraid of what people will think of you and therefore you never speak up or volunteer? Are you comparing what God has given to you to what God has given to someone else in an unhealthy way? Don't waste another day avoiding the opportunities in front of you to faithfully use what God has given to you to bring Him glory and point others to how awesome He is.

Matthew 25:14–30

Parable of the talents.

Exodus 35

All the women who were skilled in sewing and spinning used their skills.

Exodus 36

God gave men the certain skill and wisdom to perform tasks involving the building of the sanctuary.

II Chronicles 2

A talented craftsman majorly contributed to the building of the Temple.

Here, we see the parable discussed in the devo as well as times where God was building something important, and He used the skills and abilities He had given the people to accomplish the task at hand. From sewers to spinners to craftsman, God used them all. What has God made you good at? He desires to use you to build His kingdom.

RESPONSE QUESTIONS

What are the things you are really good at?

Do you sometimes neglect working on these talents? If so, why?

Do you see your talents differently knowing that God entrusted you with them?

How is it that you can use your talents for the glory of God?

Colossians 3:23 (NIV) says, "Whatever you do, work at it with all your heart, as working for the Lord." When we have the goal of doing everything for the Lord, this desire will overflow into what we are doing.

Go do something that you love and enjoy today! If it's cooking, then cook. If it's drawing or painting, then draw or paint. If it's running or biking, then go outside and run or bike. If it's writing or singing, then go write or sing. If it's gardening or photography, then garden or take pictures! As you are doing this thing you love and enjoy, talk with God. Thank Him for giving you the ability to do what you love and ask Him to show you how He intends for you to do it for His glory.

At the end of your day, return to this page and journal about how it went. Journal about how you were encouraged to use your talents and what you love for the glory of God.

you are understood

Life is tough and happy. It consists of many questions, lots of laughter, several tears, some unexpected news, and handfuls of different emotions. To be a human in this life is to experience quite a bit. I know for me it is always so relieving to process all these different things out loud with a friend who gets it. Even as I am writing this book, it is so comforting to reach out to my mom and hear her say that she understands what I am experiencing. I think we can all agree that it's comforting to do life alongside somebody who understands and can relate. To navigate through times that are hard with someone who wants to walk with me makes the walking easier. To verbalize to someone in a safe space what I'm overthinking in my head makes me feel not so crazy. To celebrate what went well next to someone who rejoices with me makes the celebration even sweeter than before.

Every single person desires to be understood, but for some reason, our initial response isn't to lean into the God of all-understanding. Sometimes we very easily find ourselves thinking of God as being far away and because He is perfect, maybe He doesn't understand the imperfect realities of being a human. If you relate to feeling this way, be encouraged that Jesus is the greatest friend who relates to us more than we may realize.

Jesus is the friend who not only walks alongside us through the tough stuff, but He was fully human on earth and walked through the tough stuff too. He really does understand. Jesus is the friend who had all the hard moments to think through, and He relates to us as we learn how to sort out our minds when we are in our heads. He had joyous moments of celebration and really does share in our gladness. He gets it. He was tempted in every way as you and I are. He had questions and received heartbreaking news. He lost loved ones and processed through every emotion. We don't acknowledge the humanity of Jesus often enough, and therefore we forget how understanding and relatable He actually is.

A question I love to ask Jesus is, "How did You respond to feeling this way?" Jesus set the perfect example of how we are to walk through life, but He didn't set the perfect example in a perfect world. He set the perfect example amid the same broken world that you and I both walk in. This is a cause for relief and even more of an eagerness to call upon His Name and trust Him. Not only did He bring a means of salvation to all who believe in Him, but He is the best friend who is closer than a brother whom we all long for.

Hebrews 4

Empathizes with our weaknesses.

I Corinthians 10:13

Not tempted beyond what is common to man.

Philippians 2

Humbled himself and became a human being.
He was hungry (fasting), he was tired (woman at the well & sleeping on a boat in a storm), he got sad (cried after lazuras died), he felt anxious (sweating blood before being arrested before the crucifixion)...
Jesus gets it.

RESPONSE QUESTIONS

Look up the following verses and write out the human qualities you see that Jesus had.

John 11:35

John 4:6 + Mark 4:38

Matthew 26:37–39

Mark 11:12 + Matthew 4:2

John 15:11

Not only this, but Jesus knew what it was like to be disliked, to be betrayed, to be questioned, to lose a loved one, to get frustrated, and so forth. He had siblings and close friends. He was filled with joy and even celebrated at a wedding! He really was fully God and fully man.

What does it say about Jesus that He would be like us and empathize with us in our weaknesses?

Knowing this, how do you see your relationship with God differently? Does it help you come before Him with your life and all that it entails, now knowing that He understands?

Write out below what you are feeling right now or what it is that you are going through

Now, God says that we can boldly approach His throne of grace and ask for help in our time of need, so share with God what you wrote above. Ask Him to help you and encourage you. Tell Him what you need and present your requests before Him. Thank Him and declare or write down how good and faithful and empathetic He is. Reminding yourself of the character of God will help you find level ground when going through life's daily things that can so easily distract us from who He is. (Hebrews 4:16; Philippians 4:6–7)

you are worth it

I had a plant that I named Penelope my junior year of college. She was a lovely golden pothos plant that hung from my ceiling and sat in a pretty pot. She was my first plant that I owned and cared for. About six months into having this plant, I was studying on my bed and suddenly heard this loud bang on my nightstand right next to me. Startled, I looked over to see that Penelope had fallen and was rolling off my nightstand. Right before my eyes she and the pot made their way to the floor and crashed. It was like a murder scene. Mud had somehow smeared across my wall, dirt covered my nightstand, the pot shattered on my floor, and Penelope just lay there. I was so sad. I called Josh (my fiancé at the time) to break the news, I called my mom and dad to tell them, and I called my Aunt Christy who is a plant expert who had helped me find Penelope and taught me how to take care of her. I was devastated. This may sound silly to have such a reaction to a plant falling, but goodness, I truly enjoyed this plant.

One of my best friends looked at Penelope's root system and told me that it was salvageable through propagating from the roots that were still intact. She said that if I put the roots in a new pot soon enough, then Penelope could most definitely be saved! I was so relieved.

I honestly think that we are all quite a lot like Penelope. We all have fallen. We all have been broken through our rebellion against the Lord, and we have all lain in the lowest place with no strength or hope of being put back together on our own. If you think about it, Penelope in no way could have stayed there on my wooden floor with no water and survived. In the same way, in our brokenness apart from the Lord, there is no way a single one of us could survive on our own.

But God in His kindness and love saw you and me worth being picked up, cared for, and put back together. Just as it broke my heart to see Penelope fall because I enjoyed her, so did it break the heart of God to see us fall from Him because He enjoys being in a relationship with each of us. Just as I rejoiced at the news that Penelope was salvageable, God rejoices at the sight of our lives, our hearts, our souls being saved by His kindness through the gift of His one and only Son, Jesus.

DIVE DEEPER INTO SCRIPTURE

As you read the Scriptures below think about how we have fallen and crashed.

Isaiah 53:6 | Isaiah 59:2 | Romans 3:23 | James 4:17

These are just a handful of verses that point to the fact that all of us really are like Penelope in that we have fallen. We all have been disobedient to God, and it has led us to be separated from Him. Not one of us are outside of this reality.

As you read the Scriptures below think about how God has saved us.

Ephesians 2:8 | John 3:16 | Romans 5:8

Just as my best friend showed me a way to save Penelope through propagation from the salvageable root system, God has shown us a way to be saved through the death, burial, and resurrection of His one and only Son, Jesus. He saw us worth making a way for.

RESPONSE QUESTIONS

Are you aware that you have fallen because of sin?

According to the verses above, how can you be saved from your sin that leads to death?

What does it say about how much you mean to God that He would send His one and only Son so that through your faith, He may be with you and you with Him forever?

Describe how it feels knowing that God saw you worth saving before you were even born.

*Go to the store today and buy a plant.
Penelope is a golden pothos, and those plants are so easy to take care
of! If you think you don't have a green thumb, that may be your starter.
Draw your plant and give it a name!*

*As you tend to your new little plant friend, remember my plant Penelope, and may
this lead you to think on the power of God's kindness to see you worth picking up and
saving. What an awesome God He is. He has the best green thumb of anyone because we
humans are such cooperative plants all the time—ha!*

You are a Seeker

There are about 4,200 different religions practiced across the world. This isn't a number showing the amount of people devoted to one religion but rather the number of religions people across the nations are devoting themselves to. From Christianity to Hinduism to Islam to Buddhism, there are people all over the globe seeking for order and purpose in their world. They are seeking for hope beyond what they can see and meaning in the place they are in. According to the Merriam Webster Dictionary, to worship is "to honor or show reverence for as a divine being or supernatural power." The fact that about 4,200 religions are practiced to express worship shows that all of us, no matter who we are or where we come from, were made to worship something greater than us.

One morning while reading in Matthew 7, I came across something that Jesus said that really got me thinking about what we are seeking and where we are expecting to find that which we are seeking. What Jesus said was, "Ask and it will be given to you; seek and you will find; knock and the door will be opened to you. For everyone who asks receives; the one who seeks finds; and to the one who knocks, the door will be opened" (Matthew 7:7–8 NIV).

All of us on earth are seeking peace and joy and purpose. Each of us are seeking confidence in identity (probably the reason that you chose to pick up this book). So, the question is not whether we are all seeking these things but rather where are we seeking to find these things? We seek these things in our relationships, in the jobs we have, in approval from others, in how fit our bodies can be, in how put together our families can look, in how much money our bank can hold, and the list goes on and on. But if we were to honestly ask ourselves how seeking real peace and joy and purpose in all those things is going, would we confidently say that it's going well?

I can say through my experience of seeking peace in approval from people or seeking joy in trying to perform at a certain level that I never find the deepest contentment and rest that my soul is craving through seeking peace and joy in those places. But when I have sought the Lord, I have found peace. When I have knocked at His door, I discovered the door that leads to joy. When I have asked Him, He has answered me with hope. When I have sought His face in trust, I have discovered a confidence that was deeply rooted. You were made for all the peace and love and purpose that you are seeking, but you will only find it in the way you were designed to when you seek the One Who made you, when you seek the One who is the Good Shepherd and who promises that in Him you lack no good thing (Psalm 23:1). We were all made to worship, but until we wholeheartedly worship the Lord, we will not find what our souls are after.

Jeremiah 29:13 | Psalm 23:1
Matthew 7:7 | Psalm 34:10

See how it is indeed a beautiful and healthy thing to seek confidence and purpose and peace and joy and rest and things such as these that we all crave. But, now we see where it is that we will actually find what we are seeking and be forever satisfied.

RESPONSE QUESTIONS

If you could describe what you are seeking in one word, what would it be?
It could be confidence, contentment, belonging, peace, joy, etc.

Where have you been trying to find that thing?

Have you found what you are seeking in the places you have been looking?

Knowing that God promises we lack no good thing in Him,
how are you going to seek differently moving forward?

What was the one word you used to describe what it is you are seeking? Was it peace or joy or belonging? I have selected many different verses below specifically addressing how we can find each of these things in the Lord. I challenge you to pick one and determine in your heart to memorize it. You could memorize it by writing it on a sticky note and putting that sticky note on your bathroom mirror. Or you could memorize it by writing out the first letter of each word on your hand so you can be challenged to recall the verse throughout the day. Whatever memorizing technique you choose, I challenge you to commit to hiding this verse in your heart. Then, when you find yourself seeking this thing in something other than God, you will remember this verse and be reminded to seek the Lord instead.

JOY	*I Peter 1:8–9* | *Psalm 16:11* | *John 15:11* *Psalm 4:7* | *I Chronicles 16:27*
PEACE	*John 16:33* | *II Thessalonians 3:16* | *Isaiah 26:3* *Philippians 4:6–7* | *John 14:27*
PURPOSE	*Romans 8:28* | *Psalm 138:8* *Job 42:2* | *Esther 4:14*
FREEDOM	*John 8:32* | *John 8:36* | *Galatians 5:1* *II Corinthians 3:17* | *Psalm 118:5*
HOPE	*Romans 15:13* | *Hebrews 6:19* *Lamentations 3:24* | *Hebrews 10:23*
CONFIDENCE	*Hebrews 10:35* | *Jeremiah 17:7* *Psalm 139:13–14* | *II Timothy 1:7*
REST	*Matthew 11:28-30* | *Exodus 33:14* | *Psalm 23:2* *I Peter 5:7* | *Psalm 91:1*
LOVE	*John 3:16* | *Romans 5:8* *Romans 8:37–39* | *Zephaniah 3:17*

You are beautiful

You are not alone whatsoever when it comes to being your own worst critic or negatively giving attention to the things about yourself you would love to change. For some of us, we simply have a hard time believing the statement "you are beautiful." I think it is safe to say that every single woman on the planet has battled this same thing in some way. May this realization that you are not alone in battling this bring you comfort, but at the same time do not allow it to be the reason you justify why you can stay in this posture of criticism and insecurity. You were never meant to stay in this place. God never desired for you to even enter this place of criticism toward the very thing He says is "fearfully and wonderfully made" (Psalm 139:14).

I remember on my wedding day how beautiful I felt, and a big reason I felt that way was because of all my bridesmaids who covered me with kind words and encouraged everything about me. It was like wherever they were was an affirmation station. They took pictures of me all day long and complimented anything and everything that they could find to compliment. It came across clearly that they were not going to allow room for one bit of insecurity or discouragement or any questioning whatsoever of my beauty. It was fantastic. I love those girls deeply.

I hope to be like my bridesmaids for you through this chapter today. Just as the girls were not permitting room for insecurity on my wedding day, we girls must get stubborn in refusing to permit the criticism from ourselves and the lies from the enemy to run rampant in our own minds in our day-to-day lives. Paul says in II Corinthians 10:5 that we are to take every thought captive that sets itself up against the knowledge of God and make it obedient to Christ. I can assure you, sister, that the thoughts chipping away at your trust in how God made you are not thoughts that are obedient to Christ. I knew my bridesmaids were not speaking empty words, but they were being honest with me—and that is a picture of the Lord's words to each of us. He doesn't speak of how beautiful we are to Him just for us to feel good on empty words. What He says about us He means, so each of us simply get to make the decision to trust that God means what He says about our image and beauty and value.

*As you listen to or watch the podcast episode
"You Are Beautiful," fill in the blanks as you go.*

We grow so _____ with our inner critic that we grow numb to the fact that such criticism is not how it is supposed to be.

We need to be _____ to ourselves and get _____ against the lies of the enemy and the criticism of ourselves.

*God's Word about how you are made are not words He says just to sound _____.
What _____ are you allowing room for in your head?*

RESPONSE QUESTIONS

On a scale of 1–10, how often would you say you make room for criticism and insecurity toward yourself? _____ Reflecting on that number, how often would you say that you make room for encouragement and truth toward yourself?

What is one quality or feature about yourself that you love?

What are the critical and discouraging words you believe about yourself?

What encouraging and truthful words can you replace the critical ones with? In other words, what does God say about how He made you? His Word is truth.

Because we as women tend to be more critical of ourselves, when we are made aware of areas in our life that can be healthier or stronger, we allow that good awareness to be more room for criticism instead of accepting that challenge with motivation to be the best version of ourselves. Let's not see beauty as a perfect body or else we will never enjoy the journey that health is.

Based on what the Scriptures below say, write in the mirror what is true about your beauty and value. May you believe these things more and more each time you look in the mirror. :)

Psalm 139:13–14

Ephesians 2:10

Genesis 1:27

you are influential

People may say that I am an influencer right now because I have a public platform on social media, but this doesn't mean that I wasn't an influencer before things online went viral. It also doesn't mean that I will stop being an influencer if the followers and public recognition go away. Influence is a gift that God has given to us in many different capacities. But the difference in one's capacity of influence does not equal a difference in importance of influence.

You do have influence. Whether you believe you have influence or not, you simply cannot change the incredible reality that you do. You are influencing people and making a difference in your community and in the lives of those you meet and beyond, so the question is not whether you have impact. The real question is how are you going to steward the influence that you have? Where are you going to lead those in your sphere of influence?

I love how Paul said in Acts 20:24 (NLT), "But my life is worth nothing to me unless I use it for finishing the work assigned me by the Lord Jesus—the work of telling others the Good News about the wonderful grace of God." The question here was not if Paul had influence or had a voice or had the ability to impact people. The question was how he chose to use it, and he so confidently said that his life was all about being obedient to the Lord and telling everyone about the life, death, burial, and resurrection of Jesus

Christ. He truly believed that there was no greater way for him to steward the influence entrusted to him.

In the Bible, there is a story about a woman who suffered from bleeding for twelve years. It is written that she spent all she had on care from doctors, but nothing was improving. In fact, she was getting worse. In other words, she was out of hope and out of options. But one of my favorite parts of this story is that she heard about Jesus. We are never told who it was that she heard about Jesus from or how it was that she came to hear of Him, but we do know that she heard about Him in some way, and this led to her approaching Jesus and being healed by Him. I share this story to say that we may never know who it was that told this woman about Jesus, but whoever told her about Him influenced her life in a way that changed her life.

May we not associate influence on the number of people who know our names or know what we have accomplished, but may we associate our influence with whatever task is at hand and with whomever we are in front of right now. Who knows? The person you pass by in the hallways or talk to at the grocery store could be like the bleeding woman who needs hope, and how you steward the influence you have could encourage them in greater ways than you realize.

I Corinthians 11:1 | Mark 5:25–34
Acts 20:24 | Matthew 5:14–16

RESPONSE QUESTIONS

What influence do you currently have (in your school, home, on your team, etc.)?

How do you see influence differently now knowing that it doesn't only mean having a lot of followers on Instagram?

How will you use your influence now that you know you do have influence?

Write a list of ways to use your influence to point people to Jesus (this can be through big things and small).

To have influence is to have an effect or impact on someone or something. How are you influencing your community, your home, your friendships, or your team for the better?

You are made for better

How many times have you heard rules or boundaries laid out and then felt as though the fun was drained or that you were missing out? Associating the word obedience to the word boring can be rather common, especially when it comes to faith. This is quite interesting, though, because all throughout the Bible, we can see countless times when words such as life, abundance, and freedom and so many more like these are spoken of in relation to knowing and obeying God. Even with all these amazing promises and hopeful words describing the commands that God gives us, we so often think that following His commands will cause us to miss out on the fun and good experiences in life.

Maybe we think that we will miss out on the fun if we are obedient to God's Word because we as humans simply like to do things our way and we believe we know what's best. Or we may be convinced that God is holding out on us and doesn't have our best interest in mind. Another reason we avoid obeying God could be because we know people who claim to be Christians who spoke about following God in a boring, no-fun kind of way, and this painted for us a picture of what Christianity must be.

In Psalm 19, David describes the Word of God to be sweeter than honey and radiant, bringing light to the eyes. And in Psalm 34:8 (NIV), David says to "taste and see that the Lord is good; blessed is the one who takes refuge in Him." Whatever the reason you have turned down the idea of obeying God's Word is, see these verses as an invitation and as a promise. You are invited to taste the sweetness of God's Word and to see the light and the clarity that He gives. You are being invited to genuinely know who He is. By following Him and applying what He says to your life, you are promised to have a better life than what you could have ever accomplished on your own. God promises in His Word that His way is better, but we will not experience this better way of life through avoiding obedience to His Word.

I am not saying that obedience to God always feels like the better choice, nor am I saying that everybody will think you are a cool and fun person when you are obedient to God. This is simply because obedience to God is not popular in the world and requires saying no to things that appear to be the best in the moment. What I am saying, though, is that there is a deeper satisfaction and a greater joy when we walk in obedience to the Lord— because this way of walking is what we were made for, and as you taste it and see it, you will discover that it's better.

Psalm 34:8 | Psalm 19:10
Isaiah 55:8–9 | Proverbs 3:5–6 | I John 5:3

RESPONSE QUESTIONS

Do you think you will miss out on the fun or the best parts of life if you obey God?

Why is that?

*How will you respond to the invitation from God
to taste His Word and see that it is good?*

Do you trust that God's way will be better than anything this world can offer?

What is your favorite sport?

_____

Now write out the rules that are in this sport.

Take note of how this sport is your favorite and how an important part of what makes this sport great are the rules that it holds. The rules allow for structure and order, and they make the game BETTER. In a similar but deeper way, the instruction and commands of the Lord bring order to our lives. They are trustworthy, and they make our lives BETTER. You were made for better.

You are made for freedom

It was a super pretty, blue sky kind of day, and while on my way outside, I saw a bird that couldn't seem to find its way out of the garage. I tried to help by opening the big garage door for my little bird friend, but to my amazement, even with the wide-open space that the bird had to happily fly away, it continued to fly into a closed window inside of the garage! There was a clear pathway to be free, but the little bird kept going in a direction proven to be unhelpful that left the bird in the same place.

I think we can all relate in some way to this bird. We are, or we have been, stuck in habits of fearful and worrisome thinking. We keep flying into windows of addictions and patterns that keep proving themselves to be unhelpful in our lives. Like the bird stuck in the garage but flying in every direction except the wide-open door, we are giving so much energy to finding freedom, but the direction we are going simply isn't working—and it's leaving us in the same place of shame, frustration, and defeat repeatedly. All the while, a huge door has been opened for us, and all we need to do is change direction and move forward. The bird so badly wanted to be free, and it had complete access to be free. In the same way, we are craving the very freedom that we were made for and have total access to.

Jesus said in John 10:9–10 (NKJV), "I am the door. If anyone enters by Me, he will be saved, and will go in and out and find pasture. . . . I have come that they may have life, and that they may have it more abundantly." I love how Jesus gives us pictures through His words so that we can grasp even more of who He is and what He has done for us. Reading these verses make me think of Jesus as the garage door! It is only through Him that we can get out of our captivity and be united with the Father and experience the abundant life and freedom that He made us to enjoy.

John 8:32 (NIV) says that "you will know the truth, and the truth will set you free." Notice that before being set free, we must know what the truth is. This requires us to humbly acknowledge that the way we have been trying to find freedom on our own hasn't been working, just as the way the bird was trying to get out wasn't working. We must first realize that there is a better way to go about life than the way we have been living. Jesus says in John 14:6 that He is the Truth. This means that before being set free, we need to know Jesus because He is the garage door. He sets us free from the life of bondage that we were not made to live in. He sets us free from the barrier that separates us from the Father. We are all like the bird. We all have our own garages of shame and frustration and unhelpful habits. But, like the bird, we all have total access to the way out, to the way of freedom—and that is through Jesus.

John 10:9–10 | *John 8:32*
John 14:6 | *Galatians 5:1*

LISTEN AND RESPOND

As you listen to or watch the podcast episode
"You Are Made for Freedom," fill in the blanks as you go.

Stop _____ your energy looking for freedom in every place other than Christ.

The first step toward _____ is having the awareness that we are stuck.
_____ wants you to be free!

That garage of habits, patterns, and mindsets isn't where you have to _____.

RESPONSE QUESTIONS

What garage have you been in—what habits or patterns have been keeping you stuck?

Have you been trying to find freedom from these patterns on your own?

Where has it brought you?

What does it say about God that He would know the beauty of freedom and desire for us to experience it?

MEMORIZE THE FOLLOWING VERSE

"Then you will know the truth, and the truth will set you free."

JOHN 8:32 NIV

you are made for friendship

The year before getting married, I lived in a house with some of my best girlfriends. I am convinced it was one of my best decisions and sweetest gifts. I remember going to an early-morning workout, and when I came back home and opened my mini fridge, I saw one of the other girls had left a sticky note in there for me. On it she wrote, *I am very proud of you for waking up this early! Getting that wedding bod! *heart eyes** It was such a simple thing that probably took her a minute, max, but it encouraged me so much! I remember baking cookies countless times, eating supper on our porch, having many cherished conversations, painting each other's nails, waiting up to hear how one of the girl's dates went . . . I could keep going. There were definitely tears shed and super hard conversations and miscommunication during that year too, but it all sharpened us. That year was living proof to me that people are made for friendship. We were made to do life with others and not go about this journey by ourselves. We were made to walk with people. The right friends help us when we are down and make us stronger than when we are alone.

You may be reading this and think, Wow, that sounds like a dream, but that has never been my experience with friends. That's not realistic for me. And that makes total sense that you would feel that way if that's not what your friendships have looked like for you. Maybe you have walked through nothing but drama and gossip. Maybe you have felt a lot of rejection in your past friendships, and it has seemed as though your ability to trust has been depleted. Or, maybe you have a history of not being the best kind of friend. Friendships are not easy, but no matter what your experience has been, you were made to have a friend and to be a friend.

I love this quote from Winnie the Pooh, "You can't stay in your corner of the Forest waiting for others to come to you. You have to go them sometimes." This encourages us away from thinking that we have no part to play in healthy friendships being a part of our lives. Jesus said that we are to treat others the way we would like to be treated, and regarding friendship that can look like being the quality of friend that you desire to have.

Because we are made for friendship, we cannot let our past experiences rob us from today's opportunities of friendship. Whether we have not had the best of friends or been the best friend to others, today is the day to begin being the kind of friend God calls us to be.

Proverbs 17:17 | Proverbs 27:17
Ecclesiastes 4:9–12

RESPONSE QUESTIONS

To be a quality friend is to be a friend who is kind and selfless.
It is to be a friend who is patient and thoughtful.
A quality friend loves like Jesus first loved us.

Do you have quality friends? Are you a quality friend?

If friendship is a sensitive subject in your life, write down why that is.
Maybe you're experiencing rejection. Maybe your current friends gossip all the time.
Maybe you're feeling lonely. Maybe your friends have told you that you haven't
been the best kind of friend. Have you prayed about these things or processed
these things honestly?

Do you see the value and importance of friendship differently
knowing that God made us for friendship and community?

Write out a list of ways that you can be a quality friend.

You are made for joy

Many of us have heard Bible verses that say to "rejoice always" (I Thessalonians 5:16) and "consider it all joy" (James 1:2). And, at times, it can be easy to see these commands as utterly impossible to live out because we associate joy with happiness and no human is happy every single second of their entire life. With this understanding in mind, we may ask the question, "How can I be both joyful always and honest about what I'm feeling?" Through these verses about joy, God is not saying to avoid or suppress every feeling that isn't a happy one because that wouldn't be realistic. Understanding more of what God means comes with knowing that joy and happiness are not the same thing. Happiness is an emotion experienced when something good or exciting happens, just as sadness is an emotion experienced when something upsetting takes place. Joy, however, is a deeper cheerfulness that remains even during tough things, and it is found when we are filled with the Holy Spirit through faith in Jesus.

I have come to find that when I am focused on God, I am fully occupied with joy even when it really doesn't make sense to be due to whatever it is I may be going through. This can only be because of something stronger than my temporary circumstances. The Lord is joy, and therefore to know Him is to be filled with and strengthened by joy. As Elisabeth Elliot said so well, "The secret is Christ in me, not me in a different set of circumstances."

You and I were made for a deeply rooted joy, but to experience the strength of joy, we must be patient as we discipline ourselves to practice choosing joy. Anything we want to get good at, we must invest time into, so in the same way, we must invest time into practicing how to choose joy. We must practice focusing on God. We must practice considering each moment as pure joy. Jesus talks about how our lives are fruitful when we fix our focus on Him, and some of this fruit He is referring to is joy. We must practice processing through the very real emotions we are feeling and being honest about them, but ultimately allowing God to guide us and dictate what next steps we take. The more we practice focusing on God, the stronger this muscle of choosing joy gets and the more we realize that we were in fact made for joy.

Nehemiah 8:10 | 1 Peter 1:8–9
Psalm 16:11

ELISABETH ELLIOT

*"The secret is Christ in me,
not me in a different set of circumstances."*

RESPONSE QUESTIONS

*Describe how you feel knowing that "rejoice always" does not mean
to pretend being happy always? Do you feel relieved knowing this?
Do you have a better understanding now?*

*Does it feel more tangible to choose joy knowing that
choosing joy comes from seeking God?*

Write about a time you intentionally chose joy.

I once read an article about how joy and gratitude are basically best friends. When we practice being grateful, joy comes with it— and vice versa. Fill out the Polaroid pictures below with writings or drawings of things you are grateful for!

You are made for peace

While in premarital counseling, our counselors showed Josh and me a passage in Mark 7 where Jesus was approached by some of the religious leaders. They asked Him why His disciples didn't wash their hands as the Jewish law instructed. Jesus responded to them boldly. There is so much to talk about from this passage, but our counselors advised us to go sit by ourselves to pray and reflect on how Jesus responded in that moment, how He may have felt, and what He may have faced in that conversation.

As I did, I was amazed as I realized the moment of intense conflict that Jesus was in during this story. He was with His disciples and then suddenly was approached by these men who clearly disagreed with Him. I felt so understood in this moment as I thought about how Scripture says that Jesus was tempted in every way, but He did not sin (Hebrews 4:15). If Jesus was tempted in every way, then like me, He was probably tempted in this moment before responding to keep everyone happy and find some way to make sure that everyone agreed, thinking that this was the only way He could be at peace. I know that I have been tempted to be timid in communicating something due to the fear that the peace would be disturbed if I said something conflicting. Knowing that Jesus was in a conflicting moment, was probably tempted to people-please, and still chose to speak the truth with love and boldness anyway, encouraged me to know that the presence of conflict doesn't have to mean the absence of peace. In other words, my peace is not hanging on my ability to keep everyone happy, and this is a great thing because the expectation for me to keep everyone happy is an unattainable one.

Elisabeth Elliot said it so well—"Fear arises when we imagine that everything depends on us." In other words, our peace is robbed when we are convinced that keeping everyone okay and happy is our job. Jesus knew His job and He knew where peace came from. His job was to glorify the Father, and His peace came from the Father. Knowing that our peace comes from God and not our circumstances allows us to remain calm and then be somebody who operates out of true peace in any circumstance to help and bless those around us. Because if our inner peace is robbed anytime there is conflict, then how can we be peacemakers in the midst of the conflict? We can't because we would be so consumed with the conflict within ourselves. I will encourage it again—the presence of conflict doesn't have to mean the absence of peace.

peace

to join (eiro); by implication prosperity
one, quietness, rest, + set at one again

DIVE DEEPER INTO SCRIPTURE

Isaiah 26:3 | Matthew 5:9 | Philippians 4:6–7 | Romans 12:18 | Colossians 3:15 | John 14:7

RESPONSE QUESTIONS

Have you ever felt like peace was absent because conflict was present?

*Have you ever felt the pressure of keeping everyone happy all the time?
Describe the weight that this pressure is on you.*

*True, lasting peace is found through trusting in God. What are practical ways you can
trust God today and in turn have peace through any circumstance?*

*In what ways do you think you would be a better peacemaker if you truly believed that
peace doesn't have to be absent in the presence of conflict?*

Have a plan of action for the next time there is conflict within yourself or with someone else. If peace is found through trusting in God, then pray about how you can trust the Lord the next time conflict arises. Ask God to show you the places you aren't trusting Him and ask Him to help you and to strengthen your trust in Him when it comes to conflict.

Identify the fears and doubts and anxieties that run through your mind when there is conflict. What I mean by this is, what are the thoughts that fill your mind when in an uncomfortable or conflicting setting? Write them below.

O

O

O

O

Next time, instead of letting those things take the lead, practice trusting God by leaning on His Word. Commit to memorizing one or all of these verses below so they may be hidden in your heart and ready to call to mind whenever conflict approaches.

Isaiah 26:3 | Philippians 4:6–7
Matthew 5:9 | Colossians 3:15 | John 14:27

Even if you need to have simple statements to recall in those times of conflict, find a statement such as the examples below to remind yourself of when it's easy to forget.

It is not my job to keep everybody happy.
The presence of conflict doesn't mean the absence of peace.
I am okay, and the world is not crashing down.

You are made to be holy

To be holy is to be without flaw. It is to be pure, and it is to be set apart from the way that the world operates. Jackie Hill Perry said it well when she said to "look to God for understanding of what holiness is" because God is the One calling us to be holy, and He Himself is holy. For God is totally pure and perfectly good and absolutely complete in and of Himself. We are called to be holy because we are called to be in right relationship with God, and we cannot have a right relationship with God apart from holiness.

The Lord says for us to be holy as He is holy, but it doesn't take long to look at who God is and look at what holiness means and be certain that as people we are incapable on our own of even coming close to being holy as God calls us to be. We cannot be holy on our own strength or by our own good deeds or by striving to earn a certain reputation. It is only through repentance of our sins and faith in Jesus that we can be made holy as God is holy. Through Christ I am made holy, and it is through being filled with His Spirit that I can daily live out what it means to be holy. The Lord is so kind that He would provide a way for us to be made pure and perfect in His eyes and reveal to us who He is and how we are to live out this command of holiness.

People see the Lord through us living out holiness because the Lord lives in us who have been saved. When we think about the fruit of the Holy Spirit, we think of love, joy, peace, patience, kindness, goodness, gentleness, faithfulness, and self-control (Galatians 5:22–23). Therefore, to be filled with the Holy Spirit is to be filled with these things, and when people see these things in our life, they are seeing the Lord. Paul says in Romans 12:2 (ESV), "Do not be conformed to this world, but be transformed by the renewal of your mind, that by testing you may discern what is the will of God, what is good and acceptable and perfect." By choosing to walk in holiness (not conforming to the ways of the world), we discover that the will of God is the best and that He is the best. We discover that pursuing holiness daily is what we were made for because to pursue holiness is to pursue God. The more we pursue God, the more we grow to know God, and therefore, the more we grow in the likeness of who God is. With this said, the more we grow in the likeness of who God is, the more others see Him in our lives and are encouraged to know Him personally too.

holy

to be a 'saint'; sacred; (physical, pure moral blameless)
to live differently/set apart
"consecrate" is to be 'dedicated'; innocent; set aside

DIVE DEEPER INTO SCRIPTURE

I Peter 1:15-16 | *I Corinthians 6:19–20* | *I Corinthians 3:16–17*
I Peter 2:9 | *Revelation 4:8* | *Hebrews 12:14* | *Ezekiel 43:12*

RESPONSE QUESTIONS

What does it mean to be holy?

Why is it so important for us to be holy as God is holy?
How is it possible for us to be holy as God is holy?

Knowing that other people can see God in us through our pursuit of holiness,
how does this encourage you to be intentional in how you live?

If pursuing holiness means to pursue God, we must be disciplined and intentional in our daily pursuit of knowing who God is and drawing near to Him (James 4:8). It is not a surface level behavior modification, but it is a transformed life from the inside out and a day-by-day working out of our salvation with fear and trembling (Philippians 2:12). Remember, we are made holy before God by the work of Jesus, not by our own works, but to live out this holiness is a day-by-day choice to walk in step with the Holy Spirit who now lives inside of us.

Fill out the Polaroid pictures with different ways you can pursue God and grow in holiness through a real pursuit of Him this week.

You are made to keep going

Growing up, soccer was my sport. I loved everything about the game, and I still do. Something I will never forget were the months of training and intense conditioning leading up to the start of the new season. These months were full of sprints, sprints, and more sprints. They were full of workouts that made my lungs burn and made me sweat so much it was like I had jumped in a pool. It consisted of pushups and weightlifting and did I mention sprints? Those were some tiring hours, but I remember being so hyped up when thinking about how ready our team would be when it was time to play. I remember thinking about how the training hours day in and day out would prove themselves to be worth it. I remember thinking about how grateful I would be that I worked hard then, so that I would be faster, stronger, and more equipped when it was go-time on the field.

Life can be a lot like this in certain ways. There are days where we feel like the day-to-day tasks require a lot of grit because they are hard and tiring, but when we think about why we are doing that difficult thing, it is as though we are energized to keep going. Just as I was energized to keep training when I would think about the games coming up and how worth it all the effort was, so are we energized and hyped up to keep being faithful to God when we think about how worthy He is and how sweet the day will be when we see Him face to face and hear the words, "well done, my good and faithful servant." Even Jesus was encouraged to endure the cross as He looked ahead to the joy that was set before Him.

There are so many times throughout Scripture where we are told to seek the Lord and look to His face and consider who He is and fix our eyes on Him. I believe one of the greatest reasons this is, is because God knows that when our focus is on things other than Him, we can easily forget why we are training. When we forget our reason for being obedient to Him and faithfully showing up each day, we can easily grow weary. Just as I was encouraged during the hard days of training when I remembered why I was training, you too will be encouraged during the hard days of life when you remember who God is and why you are living for Him.

weary

to give up, become discouraged, lose heart

DIVE DEEPER INTO SCRIPTURE

Galatians 6:9 | *Colossians 3:2*
II Timothy 4:7 | *Hebrews 12:1–2*
II Thessalonians 3:13

RESPONSE QUESTIONS

In what areas of your life have you been tired lately and in need of energy?

Describe a time that you began to grow tired and weary in following God because you took your focus off of Him and got distracted by other things.

Describe a time that you focused on God and grew encouraged to keep going.

What does it say about God that looking to Him would bring
encouragement and energy to keep going?

_____

_____

_____

As mentioned in the devo, we are encouraged to keep going when we remember why we began in the first place. You may not be tired or weary right now, but we all have those days. And when those days come, we need encouragement. Write down below why it is that you follow God. Write down why you spend time in His Word and work wholeheartedly to honor His Name. Write down why you choose to love people even when it's hard, why you spend time in prayer, why you memorize Scripture, why you keep serving in your community, etc.

This is my "why"

_____

_____

_____

Go do something challenging, maybe it's writing a poem or walking a mile or telling someone how you truly feel about them today, and after you finish, journal about—

how you felt when you were done.

_____

how you felt knowing that you accomplished it.

_____

what motivated you to keep going.

_____

You are made to love people

When I was fourteen years old, I surrendered my life to the Lord and took ownership of my own faith in Christ. This happened right before my fifteenth birthday, and I had an uncontainable and deep desire to love people. So, I asked my peers in school to participate in fifteen acts of kindness. When my teacher became aware of this, he added to it and told the students that if they participated in fifteen acts of kindness, then they would receive ten bonus points for their grade in that class. I then got invited to speak to the entire student body over the intercom one morning to invite them to join me in fifteen intentional acts of kindness. It was such a beautiful thing to have my peers approach me throughout the day, telling me the acts of kindness they had done.

I share this with you because sometimes we can overcomplicate what it means to love people because we overlook our day-to-day encounters with people. It truly is making the most of the opportunities we are given throughout our everyday lives. Holding the door open for someone, sharing a compliment while passing by someone in the grocery store, speaking kindly of someone when they aren't around, choosing to forgive a wrong done to you,

praying for somebody when they come to your mind, buying a gift for somebody just because, giving someone a call to simply see how their day is going . . . the list goes on. These things mentioned are not always easy by any means, but I know that when I have acted out of love, it has always left me in a more refreshed, free, and energized place in my soul. Why? Because God is love and He made us in His image. We were made to love one another. God even says that if we claim we love God but we hate the person next to us, then we are a liar (I John 4). To love God is to love people; they go hand in hand and cannot be separated from one another.

In Donald S. Whitney's book, *Spiritual Disciplines for the Christian Life*, he defines worship as "focusing on God and responding to God," and this is a picture of living a life of love as we were designed by God to do. When we focus on who God is and the love He demonstrated for us, we respond to Him in gratitude by loving people. Jesus says that the world will know we belong to Him by our love. In other words, we show the world who God is by how we love people. It doesn't matter what their status is, what their history is, what their ethnicity is, or what their opinions are. We simply are to love them.

Matthew 22:37–39 | I John 4:19
Romans 12:9 | II Corinthians 5:14
I Corinthians 13:1–8

RESPONSE QUESTIONS

Do those around you know you belong to God by the way you love? Why or why not?

Knowing that God loved us even though we gave Him reason not to, how are you encouraged to love people even when it is hard?

What are some practical ways you can love people today?

On the previous page you wrote out some practical ways you can love people. From that list, choose one that you will commit to implementing into your day today.

When doing that act of love, think about God's love for you and why it is that you are loving that person. And remember, this is not simply the things you do that people see, but this is also how you think of them and what you say about them when they aren't around.

What is that act of love?

At the end of the day, come back and journal about how it went. Was it hard? Did they respond how you thought? Did it refresh you knowing you got to shine some light on their day?

You are made to wonder

I remember sitting in my classroom sometimes growing up, being afraid to ask a question about what the teacher was saying because I thought I was supposed to know the answer. I was afraid my classmates would think I was dumb because I didn't know.

As we grow up, there is this stigma that communicates we don't have permission to ask as many questions as we did when we were little because we think we are supposed to know all the answers now. Some of us feel as though we have passed the age that allows us to not know everything and simply wonder what something means. Like a young child who is utterly amazed at something they are hearing, some of us feel immature or silly to let ourselves get that excited. To be filled with wonder sometimes is incorrectly perceived as a lack of maturity in our world.

God made us to wonder and encourages us to keep learning and keep asking questions. He says in Philippians 1:6 that He promises to finish the good work He began in us. This tells us that our whole time here on earth is a time of growing and learning as we become more and more

like Jesus. It can be so easy to miss out on opportunities to grow and embrace the joy of learning simply because we thought we were supposed to know it all already or we felt it childish to make it known that something simple filled us with wonder.

I love in Proverbs 9:9 (ESV), where Solomon says, "Give instruction to a wise man, and he will be still wiser; teach a righteous man, and he will increase in learning." This brings such joy because it communicates that no matter how old we get or how much knowledge and insight we have attained, there is always room to grow and ask questions and be amazed. Even after Jesus told stories about the kingdom of heaven, the disciples asked Him what He meant, and He explained. To wonder and ask questions and have a desire to learn requires of us to let go of the unrealistic expectation that we are supposed to know everything already. We were made to wonder. To honestly acknowledge we do not know everything and to be filled with wonder at what we get to learn about God and life is not childish but rather quite humble—and a place where maturity grows.

Proverbs 9:9 | *Jeremiah 33:3*
Proverbs 18:15 | *II Timothy 3:16*
James 1:5 | *Luke 2:52*

RESPONSE QUESTIONS

Have you ever been afraid to admit you didn't know something?
Describe that time and why you were afraid.

Reading the verses above, are you encouraged to be excited about
learning and about asking more questions?

What does it say about God that He wants us to come to Him
with our questions and He wants us to keep learning?

By seeing questions and wonder and learning in a new light, do you feel like it will be
easier for you to freely ask questions without fear or timidity? Why or why not?

What are some questions about Scripture or life that you have had but have been afraid to ask?

Go to the Lord in prayer today and ask Him about these things. Go to someone you trust and ask them about these things. Write down how these conversations helped you.

Plus, I guarantee you that when you are bold enough to say you don't know everything, people will feel like they can relate to you more and as though they can be honest about the things that they don't know too. How cool is it that our humility and boldness help others find freedom in their life—sometimes without us even knowing it?

you are made to make Him Known

In I John 1:1–4 (NIV) one of Jesus' disciples, John, writes, "That which was from the beginning, which we have heard, which we have seen with our eyes, which we have looked at and our hands have touched—this we proclaim concerning the Word of life. The life appeared; we have seen it and testify to it, and we proclaim to you the eternal life, which was with the Father and has appeared to us. We proclaim to you what we have seen and heard, so that you also may have fellowship with us. And our fellowship is with the Father and with His Son, Jesus Christ. We write this to make our joy complete."

In the opening of this letter, John was writing about how he and other believers had been with Jesus. They heard Him, saw Him, and touched Him. They knew Jesus. John was testifying and proclaiming about the reality of their encounter and relationship with Jesus. John goes on to say that what they had seen, they are now sharing because they wanted these people to have fellowship with them. He said that it brought them complete joy to share with them and remind them about the God they had seen, heard, and touched. Now, while John is writing this letter to a group of believers to encourage them in their faith, I believe we can learn a lot from this when it comes to sharing our faith with anyone and finding joy in doing so.

There are many ways a book could end, but I could think of no better way than to encourage you in the powerful reality that you are called to also "proclaim what you have seen and heard." You are called by God on purpose to tell others about Him. You are meant to share with people about how you have personally walked with God, how you have seen Him through His Word and in your life, how you have heard Him, and how you genuinely know Him. Throughout the past twenty-nine chapters, we have been growing in confidence about who God says we are. We have been discovering the truth about who we are not, who we are, and what we were made for, and there is a hurting world all around you filled with people who don't know this. They don't know where their real identity is found. They don't know that they have purpose. They don't know who God is. The only way your friends and family and the strangers you pass by on a daily basis can know who they were truly made to be is through knowing who God is, and you have been given the purpose and opportunity to testify about who He is to them. What an honor of a responsibility!

So, with this truth and confidence in your heart, don't keep it to yourself. This truth you have been learning is meant to be shared, and God intends for you to share it. And just like John and the other early believers, your joy will be complete in doing so. Go and proclaim this hope so that others may share in this joy with you.

Matthew 28:19–20 | Mark 16:15
II Corinthians 5:20 | I John 1:1–4

RESPONSE QUESTIONS

How have you heard, seen, and touched the Lord in your life?

What are reasons that you don't share your faith with others in your life?

If one of these reasons resonate with you, commit to memorizing these verses so that they take the forefront of your mind and help you in the moments it is hard to share your faith.

Fear of what people think | Galatians 1:10; II Timothy 1:7

Outside of comfort zone | Joshua 1:9; Proverbs 3:5–6

Forgetting importance | Acts 20:24; Mark 16:15; James 1:22

Have you proclaimed and testified to others about your relationship with the Lord? If so, how have you seen your joy be made complete in sharing your faith?

*Describe how you are challenged/encouraged to make the most
of the opportunities given to you to share your faith?*

Who is someone you know who doesn't know the Lord?

*Below, write down how you would explain the Gospel and your own relationship
with God to them. Write down how you would explain to them that they can have
this relationship too.*

This is so good and exciting to journal about because God says in I Peter 3:15 that we are to always be prepared to give an answer for the hope that we have. Journaling our thoughts with God is an awesome way to intentionally prepare to share our hope in Jesus with people.

Whether you just gave your life to Jesus or you have known Him for a long time, you are called by God on purpose to share this Good News with everybody. He will strengthen you and equip you to do so, so don't be afraid. :)

*May your love for God and people drive you
to never keep this news to yourself!*

LIVE YOUR FAITH

Dear Friend,

This book was prayerfully crafted with you, the reader, in mind. Every word, every sentence, every page was thoughtfully written, designed, and packaged to encourage you—right where you are this very moment. At DaySpring, our vision is to see every person experience the life-changing message of God's love. So, as we worked through rough drafts, design changes, edits, and details, we prayed for you to deeply experience His unfailing love, indescribable peace, and pure joy. It is our sincere hope that through these Truth-filled pages your heart will be blessed, knowing that God cares about you—your desires and disappointments, your challenges and dreams.

He knows. He cares. He loves you unconditionally.

BLESSINGS!
THE DAYSPRING BOOK TEAM

Additional copies of this book and
other DaySpring titles can be purchased
at fine retailers everywhere.
Order online at dayspring.com
or
by phone at 1-877-751-4347